OREGON

Past and Present

Greg Roza

New York

Published in 2010 by The Rosen Publishing Group, Inc.
29 East 21st Street, New York, NY 10010

Library of Congress Cataloging-in-Publication Data

Roza, Greg.
Oregon: past and present / Greg Roza.—1st ed.
    p. cm.—(The United States: past and present)
Includes bibliographical references and index.
ISBN 978-1-4358-3515-3 (library binding)
ISBN 978-1-4358-8480-9 (pbk)
ISBN 978-1-4358-8481-6 (6 pack)
1. Oregon—Juvenile literature. 2. Oregon—History—Juvenile literature. I. Title.
F876.3.R69 2010
979.5—dc22

2009016193

Manufactured in the United States of America

CPSIA Compliance Information: Batch #LW10YA: For Further Information contact Rosen Publishing, New York, New York at 1-800-237-9932

On the cover: Top left: Old West homesteaders near the Klamath Indian reservation in Oregon. Top right: A worker carries flowers in Willamette Valley, Oregon. Bottom: A view of Mount Hood from Portland, Oregon.

Contents

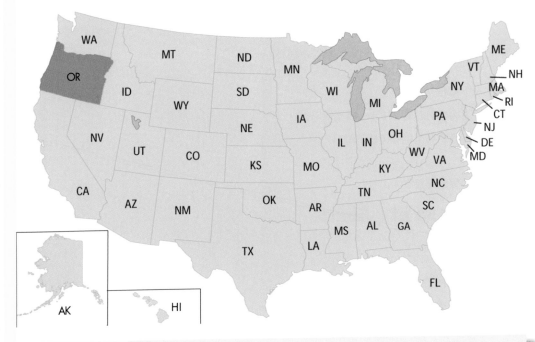

This topographic map of Oregon shows the natural features of the land, such as mountains, rivers, and lakes. The map of the United States shows where Oregon is located in the country.

Introduction

There are different stories to explain how Oregon got its name. One story says it came from the Spanish word *orejon*, which means "big-eared." According to another story, the name comes from the French word for hurricane, *ouragan*. Still others say it may have come from the Native American words for "beautiful river." Many Oregonians prefer the final story because it describes one of Oregon's finest qualities: its natural beauty.

Several years before Oregon became the thirty-third state of the Union in 1859, Judge Jessie Quinn Thornton wrote the motto *Alis volat propiis* for the Oregon Territory. *Alis volat propiis* is Latin for "She flies with her own wings." The phrase served as the motto for Oregon until 1957, when it was changed to "the Union." However, in 1987, the motto was changed back to *Alis volat propiis*. According to the Oregon Law of 1987, the motto was reclaimed because it "reflected the independent character of the Oregon pioneer settlers who established their own government."

Today, the people of Oregon pride themselves on living in one of the most progressive states in the country. Oregon is both unique and innovative—two concepts emphasized by the state's poetic motto.

Chapter 1

The Land of OREGON

Oregon is a state of remarkable beauty and diversity. It has snow-capped mountains, rich forests, deep gorges, bright deserts, lush rain forests, vast plains, and gurgling estuaries. Wind blows moist air from the Pacific Ocean over its coast. As the air hits the Cascades and Coast Range, it rises and cools. The moisture falls as rain, making western Oregon a vibrant, green region. Small pockets of rain forests can be found in the mountains there. Much of the rain that falls on the mountains forms swiftly flowing rivers that make their way back to the Pacific Ocean.

The climate is very different to the west of the Cascades and Coast Range. Once wind blows the air past the eastern mountains, it is hot and dry. Much of the eastern part of Oregon has desertlike conditions and ancient, salty lakes that are still evaporating. These two extremes make Oregon a truly fascinating place for geologists and tourists alike.

Oregon Coast

The 362-mile (583 kilometers) Pacific Coast of Oregon is 100 percent public land. Much of the coast features cliffs and rocks shaped by the pounding tidewaters of the Pacific. Dangerous waters mark many

Rock formations, such as those at Canon Beach, are common sights along the Pacific Coast of Oregon.

areas. These waters are capable of sinking ships that stray too close to the shore. However, numerous bays and inlets offer visitors plenty of places to enjoy water sports, such as sailing and surfing. Other coastal areas have beautiful beaches and sand dunes. Depoe Bay is home to a pod of whales for part of the year, making it an excellent place to go whale watching. Port Orford is the westernmost city in the continental United States.

Along the northern Pacific Coast, thick forests and hills lie within walking distance of the coastal areas. In the south, mountains of the Coast Range often end abruptly at the Pacific. The tallest mountain in the Coast Range is Mary's Peak, with an elevation of 4,101 feet

The Willamette Valley

The Willamette Valley lies east of the Coast Range. Three smaller rivers flow out of the mountains and join near Eugene to form the Willamette River, which flows north for 187 miles (301 km) before joining the Columbia River. Route 5 runs through the valley, connecting many of Oregon's largest cities, including Portland, Salem, and Eugene. The Willamette Valley is home to about 68 percent of Oregon's population. The valley is a major agricultural area in Oregon, producing berries, vegetables, and Christmas trees, among other things. The region is also the home of a thriving wine industry.

Because of its long history of floods, the Willamette Valley has excellent soil for farming. During the last ice age thousands of years ago, the constant freezing and thawing of glacial ice to the north helped bring rich volcanic soil south into the valley during cyclical flooding.

When Europeans first arrived in the Willamette Valley hundreds of years ago, the river often flooded its banks. It could grow to 1 mile (1.6 km) wide at points. When the waters receded, the flood plains were covered with a new layer of rich soil that was perfect for farming.

Starting in the mid-1800s, people began to build stone walls to keep the river from overflowing its banks during the flooding season. The riverbed was dredged in some areas to make boat travel possible, but this destroyed many ecosystems in the process.

Today, there are thirteen major dams on the river and its tributaries. This greatly affects the ability of native fish to migrate and spawn. Pollution from factories and communities on the river is also a major problem. Many people in Oregon are trying to protect and restore the valley to its former glory. The Willamette Riverkeeper is a conservation organization that is dedicated to protecting the Willamette and its wildlife.

(6,600 meters), although the average elevation of Coast Range mountains is about 1,500 feet (2,400 m). Numerous rivers flow out of the Coast Range and into the Pacific Ocean. Many of these rivers have created estuaries where plentiful wildlife—such as sandpipers, salmon, crabs, oysters, and seals—make their home. Siuslaw National Forest is a small rain forest located in the middle of the Coast Range. The Rogue River Valley is at the southwestern corner of the state.

Cascade Range

To the east of the Willamette Valley rise the majestic Cascades. This range, which extends from northern California to British Columbia, Canada, was primarily formed by the collision of two massive land plates. Over the course of millions of years, the plate beneath the Pacific Ocean was continuously forced under the plate forming the land of North America. Slowly, the land by the coast rose into the sky and volcanoes formed. These forces are still at work today, making the Cascades a volcanically active area.

At 11,249 feet (3,429 m), Mount Hood in northern Oregon is the tallest mountain in the state. It is a volcano that last erupted about two hundred years ago. Geologists think that Mount Hood could erupt again, but they doubt that an eruption would be powerful. Mount Hood's peak has twelve named glaciers and snowfields.

Crater Lake, situated in the Cascades in southern Oregon, formed about 6,850 years ago when a volcano collapsed, forming a caldera. Wizard Island is a younger volcano that formed in Crater Lake long after the original volcano collapsed. A smaller volcanic crater called the Witches Cauldron tops Crater Lake. Mount Hood and Crater Lake are two of Oregon's most magnificent natural tourist attractions.

The Cascade Mountains are a popular attraction year-round for people who love the outdoors, which makes Oregon a great destination for many types of sports.

Southwestern Oregon

The Klamath Mountains, a smaller range of mountains, stretch from southwestern Oregon to northwestern California. The tallest Klamath Mountain is Mount Ashland, at 7,533 feet (2,296 m). The northern section of this range is the Siskiyou Mountains. Much of this area features national forests and protected wilderness. North of the Siskiyou Mountains is the Rogue River Valley, an important agricultural area.

Columbia River Plateau

A wide plateau, which stretches from the Cascades in the west to the Rocky Mountains in the east, dominates northern and northwestern Oregon. The Columbia River Plateau, also known as the Columbia River Basin, was formed by one of the largest basalt lava flows ever on Earth's surface—approximately 63,300 square miles (164,000 sq km). This area is home to numerous rivers and gorges.

The Columbia River forms one of the largest breaks in the Cascade Range. It begins in British Columbia, Canada; forms much of the border between Oregon and Washington; and empties into the Pacific by the

Multnomah Falls, one of the more notable Oregon landmarks, has upper and lower cascades. Altogether, it is 620 feet (189 m) tall.

city of Astoria. Multnomah Falls is the tallest waterfall in Oregon. It offers one of the most impressive views along the Oregon side of the Columbia River.

The Deschutes and John Day rivers are the two main tributaries of the Columbia in Oregon. Water running off the eastern side of the

Cascades forms the Deschutes River. East of the John Day River are the John Day Fossil Beds, a 14,000-acre (5,700 hectares) national park that displays a remarkable record of plant and animal fossils from as far back as forty-five million years ago.

The Blue Mountains and the Wallowa Mountains are found in Oregon's northwest corner. Just beyond the Wallowa Mountains, the Snake River forms part of Oregon's eastern border. Over millions of years, the Snake River carved the Hells Canyon, which is the deepest gorge in the United States. At 8,000 feet (2,438 m), the Hells Canyon is deeper than the Grand Canyon.

The Oregon Closed Basin

Water in North America typically drains in one of three directions: to the Atlantic Ocean, to the Pacific Ocean, or to the Arctic Ocean. However, a large area of land stretching from Utah to Washington State has no natural outlet for the water it contains. This area is the Great Basin. It generally contains drier environments, including deserts, sand dunes, and grassy plains. It also features mineral-rich lakes and salt flats created by the gradual evaporation of ancient seas.

Central and southwest Oregon is a sparsely populated area made up of a smaller basin that is part of the Great Basin. It is sometimes called the Oregon Closed Basin. Much of this land is dry and rocky, but it also contains unique pockets of wildlife, including lakes, rivers, and streams stocked with fish; swamps, marshes, and other wetlands with a multitude of waterfowl; and rangeland for migrating cattle. These are the areas to which most of the water in the area drains. Although less than 1 percent of the state's population lives in this area, it is home to a wide variety of native and migrating wildlife.

Chapter 2

The History of OREGON

Experts believe that people first came to the area that is today Oregon around fifteen thousand years ago—or perhaps even thousands of years earlier. At that time, glaciers created a land bridge between Asia and North America, allowing nomads to migrate to the area. Archaeologists have found evidence of early nomads in the Oregonian deserts, including weapons and animal bones. These findings show that humans followed and hunted camels, mastodons, and mammoths for survival.

In 1938, an archaeologist named Luther Cressman found dozens of sagebrush bark sandals at an ancient volcanic crater in Lake County called Fort Rock. The sandals are between 10,500 and 9,300 years old. Fort Rock Cave was one of the earliest homes to people living in Oregon.

Early Explorers

The Spanish, sailing north along the California coast, may have been the earliest Europeans to reach the southern Oregon coast in the 1540s. In the early 1700s, Russian hunters and traders began working their way across the Aleutian Islands in search of seal furs. Spain feared that the Russian settlements would have a negative impact on their settlements in New Spain. In 1774, Spanish explorer Juan Perez became the first European to map the coast from California to modern-day British Columbia, Canada. In 1775, Spanish explorer Bruno de Hezeta stopped near the Columbia River. Many believe he was the first European to set foot in Oregon.

Robert Gray and the Columbia River

In 1788 and 1789, a sea captain from Boston named Robert Gray sailed along the coast of Oregon and traded with the Native Americans who came out to meet his ship. After sailing around the world and back to Boston, Gray set out again for Oregon.

In 1792, he came to the mouth of a large river and decided to explore it. Although he did not travel far, Gray became the first explorer to travel inland in the area that became known as the Oregon Country. He named the river after his ship, the *Columbia Rediviva*. Gray's discovery—and the discoveries of other American explorers who soon followed him—helped lend support to the United States' claim to the Oregon Country.

Lewis and Clark

In 1803, President Thomas Jefferson authorized the purchase of a large area of land in North America called the Louisiana Territory. The Louisiana Purchase more than doubled the size of the United States. Jefferson quickly organized an expedition called the Corps of Discovery to explore the new territory, as well as the Oregon Country.

Led by former army captain Meriwether Lewis and fellow officer William Clark, the Corps of Discovery left St. Louis, Missouri, in April 1804. The trip took them up the Missouri River, through the

Captain Meriwether Lewis *(right)* led the Corps of Discovery. Lewis's fellow officer William Clark *(left)* cocaptained the expedition, which opened the West to America.

Rocky Mountains, and down the Snake and Columbia rivers into the Oregon Country. They met the Nez Perce Indians, who fed them and showed them a new way to make canoes. The Corps sailed their new canoes down the Columbia River and reached the Pacific Ocean in December 1805.

Lewis and Clark collected important information about Native Americans, wildlife, and geography. They reported that the climate in Oregon was mild and the soil in the Willamette Valley was fertile. The Oregon Country had limitless furs, timber, and fish. This exciting news inspired many easterners to head west.

Native Americans in Oregon

Long before European explorers first came to the Pacific Northwest, there were several dozen Native American tribes spread across the area we call Oregon. The major groups included Shoshone, Klamath, Nez Perce, Chinook, Tillamook, and Coos, to name a few.

The arrival of Europeans meant drastic changes for Native Americans in Oregon. At first, white traders set up stores along the Columbia River and coincided peacefully with Native Americans. However, settlers soon drove the Kalapuya Indians away from the Willamette Valley. Other Native American groups experienced the same fate. Most were forced to live on reservations.

In the 1950s, the federal government instituted a program to assimilate Native Americans into the U.S. population. This program was more damaging to the tribes than it was helpful. In the 1970s, a new program was designed to help Native Americans regain sovereignty and tribal identity, and to become self-sufficient.

Today there are nine Native American tribes in Oregon, each with its own federally recognized government. Native American laws sometimes differ from state laws, and some residents don't have to pay state taxes. There are about fifty thousand Native Americans in Oregon today.

This painting is believed to have been created around the year 1800. It is a portrait of a Kalapuya Indian.

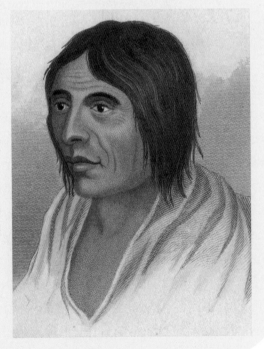

Changing Hands

In 1810, a wealthy businessman from New York named John Jacob Astor sent two expeditions to the mouth of the Columbia River. In 1811, they set up a trading settlement that became very popular with the local Native Americans. A British trading company called the Hudson Bay Company controlled the settlement and much of the surrounding coast throughout the early 1800s.

Hudson Bay employees caught salmon, set up vast farms, built lumber mills, and continued to collect beaver pelts. John McLoughlin, leader of the Hudson Bay Company in Oregon, helped new settlers and kept the peace between the British and the Americans. Today, he is remembered as the Father of Oregon.

The Oregon Trail

By the 1840s, the fur industry was declining. However, it had changed the Oregon Country significantly. Easterners rushed west to take advantage of the rich farmland, abundant forests, and fish-stocked rivers. Some easterners, such as Jason Lee, traveled to the Oregon Country for religious reasons, mainly in hopes of converting Native Americans to Christianity.

The discovery of gold in California and Oregon increased the influx of pioneers, and western settlements grew rapidly. In 1845, three thousand people traveled by land to Oregon. Many followed a route that became known as the Oregon Trail, which passed over approximately 2,000 miles (3,218 km) of rough terrain from Independence, Missouri, to Oregon City in the Willamette Valley. It was a very difficult journey. One in ten people died along the trail.

This painting, *Oregon Trail* (1869), by German artist Albert Bierstadt shows the trail in an attractive light, but the view wasn't always so inspiring to those braving its harsh conditions.

Those who made it to Oregon and other western areas had to build homes and begin farming.

The Oregon Trail was the most important route west between 1840 and 1869, the latter being the year that the first transcontinental railroad was completed. However, the trail had a devastating effect on Native Americans living in the Oregon Country. As newcomers to the state took Native Americans' food and resources, and even killed many of them with violence and disease, most were forced to flee the Willamette Valley for good.

Oregon Becomes a State

In 1846, the United States and Great Britain signed an agreement making the forty-ninth parallel north—a line of latitude in North America—the boundary between U.S. territory in the Oregon Territory and British Columbia. Finally, the United States stretched from the Atlantic to the Pacific. On February 14, 1859, Oregon became the thirty-third state in the United States.

Progress and Pollution

Starting in the second half of the 1800s, towns and cities in Oregon grew rapidly as more people moved there from the east and from Asia. Many people moved to the cities to get jobs in the new factories. Others came to work in the fishing, logging, and ranching industries. The development of railroads made traveling around Oregon easier and quicker. In 1883, a railroad was completed that connected Portland in northern Oregon to the transcontinental railroad. The trip to Oregon from eastern locations once took months of arduous travel. Now it took only weeks. Travel through the Rockies, in particular, became much easier.

In the early 1900s, the government of Oregon began building dams to create electricity and irrigation systems for farms. This had a terrible effect on the state's natural environments. Factories dumped dangerous waste in the rivers. Hillsides and mountains were stripped of forests, causing devastating landslides. By the 1960s, Oregon was one of the most polluted states. Oregon's residents spoke out for changes. By the 1970s, it had more laws protecting natural resources than any other state. Oregon was the first state to implement a bottle return law in 1971. Just as the first reports of Oregon focused on its natural beauty, its natural splendor remains a focus of its reputation today.

Chapter 3

THE GOVERNMENT OF OREGON

The Oregon state constitution was ratified in 1857. It went into effect when the U.S. Congress admitted Oregon into the Union in 1859. Like all state governments, Oregon's government is modeled after the U.S. federal government. It's made up of three branches: the executive branch, the legislative branch, and the judicial branch.

Executive Branch

Oregon's executive branch is responsible for carrying out functions that help the state run effectively. The governor of Oregon, who is elected to a four-year term, leads the executive branch. His or her duties include creating a state budget, commanding the state military, and signing bills into law. The governor can also veto laws. Oregon has had thirty-six governors since it became a state. Elected to office in 1991, Barbara Roberts was the first and only woman governor of Oregon. Ted Kulongoski became the governor in 2003 and was reelected in 2006.

Other executive branch politicians help the governor do his or her job. They include the secretary of state, treasurer, attorney general, commissioner of labor and industries, and superintendent of public

The Oregon State Capitol building, located in Salem, was built in 1938. It is the third capitol building that Oregon has had. The other two were destroyed by fire.

instruction. These officials lead state agencies that are made up of thousands of employees.

Legislative Branch

The legislative branch of Oregon government, called the Oregon Legislative Assembly, makes state laws. The legislative assembly meets at the beginning of odd-numbered years. A legislative session lasts until all issues have been dealt with. Between sessions, assembly members sit on committees and task forces designed to study issues that are likely to be discussed during the next session.

Just like the federal legislative branch, Oregon's legislature is bicameral, which means it's made up of two lawmaking bodies. The Oregon State Senate, also called the upper house, has thirty senators or representatives. Each senator represents one of the thirty districts across the state, each of which is home to about 114,000 people. Senators are elected to four-year terms.

The lower house of the legislative branch is the Oregon House of Representatives. It is made up of sixty members who each serve a two-year term. Each member represents a district made up of about fifty-seven thousand. The district lines for both the Senate and the House are redrawn every ten years to keep the numbers even.

This state seal displays images related to Oregon's history. Oxen pulling a covered wagon represent settlers who arrived along the Oregon Trail.

Judicial Branch

The system of Oregon state courts is called the Oregon Judicial System. All judges in this system are elected to one six-year term. The Oregon Supreme Court is the highest court in the state. It is made up of seven justices, currently led by Chief Justice Paul De Muniz. The only court that can modify or reverse a decision made by the Oregon Supreme Court is the U.S. Supreme Court.

Oregon Legislature

Before Oregon Country became a U.S. territory, the settlers and traders living there gathered to organize the area's first non–Native American government. Upon the death of wealthy American businessman Ewing Young, who had no known heirs, American settlers met to determine what would happen to Young's wealth. They formed a committee that attempted to create a code of laws for the Oregon Country, but failed.

In the early 1830s, Oregon settlers held a group of meetings that became known as the Champoeg Meetings in an effort to once again create a legislative body. This group had powers similar to those of the U.S. Congress, including regulating currency and creating laws. By 1848, there were twenty legislators on the committee.

When Oregon became a U.S. territory in 1848, a bicameral legislating body called the Legislative Assembly was formed. It included a nine-member council and an eighteen-member house of representatives. In 1850, the assembly passed a law moving the territorial capital from Oregon City to Salem. This caused some debate, and the move was not made official until 1851. Over the next ten years, the legislature continued to deal with problems related to constitutional changes, slavery, and boundary disputes.

When Oregon became a state in 1859, the Legislative Assembly met to organize the new state government. Over the years, the legislating body went through many changes. Perhaps William S. U'Ren initiated the most significant changes. U'Ren was a member of the House of Representatives from 1897 to 1898. He and other Oregonians believed the residents of Oregon should have a greater say in government. He championed a direct legislation program that became known as the Oregon System. This system allowed regular people to propose new laws, change the constitution, and remove politicians from office through a general election ballot measure. Today, the Oregon System is still in use and helps make Oregon one of the most progressive states in the country.

The next-highest state court, the Oregon Court of Appeals, is made up of ten judges. The chief justice appoints the chief judge, who is the head of this court. They rule on challenges to decisions made in lower state courts.

Below the court of appeals are the Oregon Circuit Courts, made up of twenty-seven trial-level district courts. Cases involving issues of taxation are settled in the Oregon Tax Court. In addition to these courts, there are nine federally recognized tribal courts in Oregon.

This document, "Oregon Territory, Willamette Settlement," is the oldest in the state's archives. It was drafted to settle cattle issues.

State Agencies

The Oregon state government sets up and maintains departments and agencies to help administer special functions related to the state's industries, businesses, people, and services. Following is a list of the most important state agencies.

- Agriculture
- Consumer and Business Services
- Corrections
- Education
- Energy
- Environmental Quality
- Fish and Wildlife
- Geology and Mineral Industries
- Human Services
- Land Conservation and Development
- Parks and Recreation
- Public Safety Standards and Training
- Revenue
- State Police
- Transportation
- Veterans' Affairs

Local and Federal Governments

Oregon has thirty-six county governments and about 240 town and city governments. A mayor and town council lead most towns. A council-manager leads most cities. A mayor and four commissioners lead the city of Portland.

Like all states in the United States, Oregon is represented by two senators in the U.S. Senate. There are five Oregon representatives in the House of Representatives.

Chapter 4

THE ECONOMY OF OREGON

As with most states, a changing global economy has mandated a shift from traditional industries in Oregon—particularly logging, agriculture, and fishing—to more modern businesses. While traditional industries still play an important role in the economy of Oregon, new industries are growing rapidly, helping the state remain competitive within the national and global economies. These new industries include service, tourism, technology, and shipping.

Let's Get Growing

Oregon is known for being a place where an abundance of crops and animals are raised. Several U.S. crops, such as hazelnuts and marionberries, are grown almost exclusively in Oregon. According to a report published by the U.S. Department of Agriculture and the Oregon Department of Agriculture, Oregon's top commodities in 2007 were nursery and greenhouse products, cattle, milk, wheat, hay, ryegrass seed, fescue seed, potatoes, Christmas trees, and onions. In addition to feeding the people of Oregon and the United States, much of Oregon's produce, beef, grains, and fish are exported to countries all over the world.

Logging in Oregon is big business, but it's still a difficult and dangerous job. Modern machinery, however, has helped to make it safer and more efficient.

Logging and Timber

Logging and timber have long been important parts of Oregon's economy. Timber is used to make lumber, plywood, particleboard, cardboard, and paper. Oregon is the nation's largest producer of Christmas trees.

Jobs in the logging and timber industries have been steadily declining for the past decade. One of the main reasons for the decline is the increased interest in environmental protection. Many Oregonians think it's important to protect Oregon's forests and wildlife, which has led to reduced logging. On the other hand, many Oregonians are in favor of increasing logging to help create jobs and boost income in rural communities. Many of Oregon's forests, including precious old-growth trees, are in protected national reserves and parks.

Fruits and Vegetables

The Willamette Valley is home to some of the most fertile and productive farmland in the world. More than 170 types of crops are cultivated in the Willamette Valley, including hay, grass, legumes, nuts, vegetables, tree fruit, berries, and grapes (many of which are used to make wine). Ninety-nine percent of the hazelnuts grown in the United States are grown in the Willamette Valley.

Pears, cherries, and other tree fruits are grown in the Rogue Valley. These crops, in addition to world-famous cherries, are also raised in the valleys around Mount Hood. Cranberries and lily bulbs are cultivated on the coast. Potatoes are grown in eastern Oregon. In southeast Oregon, the main crops include onions, potatoes, beets, and hay.

The farms of the Columbia Basin are the largest in Oregon. The size of the average farm there is 4,000 acres (1,618 hectares). Sixty percent of the wheat grown in Oregon is grown there. Other crops that are raised in the Columbia Basin include potatoes, alfalfa, carrots, onions, and corn.

Livestock and Dairy

Beef and milk are two of the state's top agricultural products. Many farms in south and southeast Oregon raise different kinds of livestock, including cows, poultry, and pigs. This area has thousands of acres of private and federal rangeland. Sheep and cattle are also raised east of the Cascades.

In the cattle industry, profits from milk production are just second to those earned from the sale of cattle and cattle products. Most of the state's dairy farms are located in western Oregon, where the land is perfect for raising cows.

Fishing

With so many streams, rivers, and lakes—not to mention miles of coast—it's no wonder that fishing has played such a large role in the state's economy. Fisheries can be found along the coast and in rivers. In 2007, the Dungeness crab business was the most profitable for Oregon. Other important

In addition to logging, Oregon is known for fishing. These crab traps and fishing ships are used at Yaquina Bay in Newport, Oregon.

species include salmon, tuna, shrimp, whiting, and oyster. In addition to commercial fishing, Oregon's abundant sources of fish provide enjoyment for many people who enjoy fishing for sport and relaxation. More than seven hundred thousand people apply for fishing licenses each year in the state.

Minerals

Gold was discovered in Oregon around the time of the 1848 California gold rush. Some individuals and companies still mine gold in eastern

Making Money in Oregon

Hundreds of years ago, Oregon's most important industries revolved around logging, fur trapping, agriculture, and fishing. Traditional industries still play an important part in Oregon's economy and provide millions of jobs. However, in Oregon, like in most states, the changing world has caused the economic emphasis to shift to more modern industries.

Today, service industries in Oregon employ more people than any other and make up about three-quarters of the gross state product. In particular, construction jobs have become more abundant in Oregon over the past decade.

Although logging and agriculture are still two of the most important industries in Oregon, they are no longer growing. Other, more modern industries are expanding instead. The state government is striving to improve the education system to attract even more technological companies to the state. Meanwhile, Oregon relies heavily on several high-profile companies, such as Nike and Intel, to help raise revenue and lower unemployment.

In recent years, Oregon has come to depend more on international shipping than ever before. A project initiated in the early 2000s to deepen the Columbia River has led to an increase in shipping traffic from Asian destinations. The project allowed the largest container ships to reach Portland, strengthening Oregon's presence in the global market.

This silicon wafer was made in an Intel factory in Hillsboro, Oregon, evidence of the growing technology business in the state.

and central Oregon. Rock collectors may also find agates, obsidians, sunstones, and thunder eggs (the state's official rock).

Oregon has become an important producer of sandstone, pumice, and gravel used in construction. Other construction materials produced in Oregon include clay, diatomite, Portland cement, and lime.

Tourism

Although much has changed in Oregon over the years, one thing remains the same: its stunning natural beauty. Tourists in Oregon can hike in pristine forests, ski on snow-capped mountains, fish in crystal-clear rivers, surf in the Pacific, dig for gold, and so much more. Oregon has about two hundred state parks and more than a dozen national forests. Tourism is also good for restaurants, stores, transportation services, hotels, and recreational companies.

Oregon has more to offer travelers than just its beauty. Historic locations include the Lewis and Clark National Historical Park in Astoria, the End of the Oregon Trail in Oregon City, and sections of the original Barlow Trail. Oregon's cities offer all the entertainment venues that one could ask for. For example, those who enjoy sports may want to see the Portland Trail Blazers tear up the court at the Rose Garden Arena. Or sports fans can watch the University of Oregon Ducks football team battle other National Collegiate Athletic Association (NCAA) teams at Autzen Stadium in Eugene. Whatever people's interests are, they are sure to find things to do in Oregon.

Chapter 5

PEOPLE FROM OREGON:
PAST AND PRESENT

In addition to its natural beauty, economic resources, and progressive government, Oregon is home to many notable people. From U.S. presidents, such as Herbert Hoover, to hit TV show creators, such as Matt Groening, Oregon has cultivated a wide array of talent. Here are some of the more recognizable names of people who call Oregon home.

Danny Ainge (1959–) Born in Eugene, Oregon, Danny Ainge was drafted by the Boston Celtics in 1981. He helped the Celtics win two championships, in 1984 and 1986. He also played for the Sacramento Kings, Portland Trail Blazers, and Phoenix Suns. In 1999, Ainge was inducted into the Oregon Sports Hall of Fame. Today, he is the president of basketball operations for the Boston Celtics.

Beverly Cleary (1916–) Beverly Cleary was born in McMinnville, Oregon. She grew up in the small farm town of Yamhill and moved to Portland to attend school. Eventually, she became a librarian in Yakima, Washington. She married Clarence Cleary, moved to California, and had twins.

Having spent so much time with children and books, it was natural for Cleary to start writing children's books. Her memorable characters, especially Ramona Quimby and Henry Huggins, have entertained children for decades.

Ann Curry (1956–) Born in Guam, Ann Curry spent much of her youth in Ashland, Oregon. In 1978, she graduated from the University of Oregon with a bachelor's degree in journalism. Her first reporting job was with a station in Medford. Shortly afterward, she was hired as a reporter in Portland. In 1997, Curry became the news anchor for NBC's *Today* show. She went on to become the host of *Dateline NBC* in 2005.

Recently, Curry reported live from African war zones in Darfur and Chad. In 2005, she toured Africa with First Lady Laura Bush to discuss the AIDS epidemic, women's rights, and education.

Matt Groening (1954–) Born and raised in Portland, Oregon, Matt Groening started drawing cartoons in high school. After college, Groening moved to Los

Cartoonist Matt Groening (pronounced GRAYN-ing) holds a likeness of his most famous creation—Bart Simpson.

Joseph The Elder and Chief Joseph

Joseph the Elder was born in the Wallowa Valley of northeastern Oregon. He was one of the first Nez Perce Indians to advocate peaceful relations with white settlers. Joseph the Elder helped set up a large reservation that stretched from Oregon to Idaho. However, when white settlers pressured the U.S. government to move Native Americans off ideal grazing and farming land, the size of the reservation was reduced to one-tenth of its original size. The Nez Perce were told that they would have to move to the much smaller reservation, which was in Idaho. Many of them moved without complaining, while others revolted. Joseph the Elder severed his ties with whites.

When Joseph the Elder died in 1871, his son Hinmuuttu-yalatlat (which translates to "Thunder Rolling Down Mountain") took his place. Whites called him Chief Joseph. Determined to avoid violence, Chief Joseph began to lead his people to the reservation in Idaho. Nonetheless, violence did erupt, and Chief Joseph was forced to lead his people into Montana to seek the help of other tribes. He had hoped to escape into Canada. However, with his people freezing and starving, Chief Joseph was forced to surrender. The Nez Perce were captured and sent to reservations in Oklahoma.

Chief Joseph became known across the country for his bravery and leadership. He died in 1904 in Washington State, far from his homeland and saddened by the state to which his people had been reduced.

Today, Chief Joseph's descendants honor him as a brave crusader for freedom and equality.

Angeles to become a writer. He sent cartoons back to Oregon for his friends and family to see. In 1980, an L.A. newspaper began publishing his cartoons.

In 1987, Groening created an animated family for the television program *The Tracy Ullman Show*. The dysfunctional family became an instant hit, and Groening was offered his very own show. After twenty years, *The Simpsons* is still as popular as ever.

Herbert Hoover led several committees and organizations that helped feed millions of starving people worldwide during World War I.

Herbert Hoover

(1874–1964) Born in Iowa, Herbert Hoover grew up in Newberg, Oregon. He moved to Salem in 1888 and worked for his uncle, learning various skills.

Hoover went to Stanford University and eventually became a mining engineer and millionaire. He served as the thirty-first U.S. president from 1929 to 1933. During his term, he helped struggling farmers, built new roads, and made "The Star-Spangled Banner" America's national anthem. When World War II (1939–1945) broke out, Hoover became involved in charitable operations all over the world.

Terri Irwin (1964–) Terri Irwin was born Terri Raines in Eugene, Oregon. Growing up, she took care of injured animals. In 1986, she started Cougar Country, a wildlife rehabilitation center.

In 1992, she married noted Australian wildlife expert and television star Steve Irwin. They spent their honeymoon filming *The Crocodile Hunter*, a documentary about the Australian outback. Together, they turned a small reptile park into the hugely popular Australia Zoo. Although a stingray killer her husband in 2006, Irwin and daughter, Bindi, continue to wow the world with exciting wildlife shows.

Dr. Linus Pauling holds a model of a molecule in his office in this photograph taken around 1960.

Ken Kesey (1935–2001) Born in Colorado, Ken Kesey was raised in Eugene and attended the University of Oregon. In 1962, his book *One Flew Over the Cuckoo's Nest* earned him worldwide recognition as one of America's finest writers. The story, which takes place in an Oregon asylum, was adapted into a popular film in 1975.

Linus Pauling (1901–1994) Born and raised in Portland, Oregon, Linus Pauling graduated from Oregon State University in 1922. After teaching at the same college, he went on to earn a Ph.D. in chemistry from the California Institute of Technology. He also studied mathematics and physics.

Pauling published hundreds of papers on numerous topics, including atoms, X-rays, vitamins, and DNA. He won the Nobel Prize in Chemistry in 1954 for his work with atoms. In 1962, he won the Nobel Peace Prize for his fight against aboveground nuclear testing and his belief in nonviolence. He is the only person to win two unshared Nobel Prizes in separate fields.

River Phoenix (1970–1993) River Phoenix was born in Madras, Oregon. He became a well-known movie actor when he starred in *Stand by Me*, released in 1986. In 1988, Phoenix was nominated for an Academy Award for his role in *Running on Empty*. His biggest role came in the 1991 movie *My Own Private Idaho*, which was mainly set in Portland. Tragically, Phoenix died of a drug overdose in 1993 at the age of twenty-three.

Timeline

1765	Major Robert Rogers first uses the word "Ouragon" in a petition to explore the American West.
1774	Spanish explorer Juan Perez maps the coast of the Pacific Northwest.
1775	Spanish explorer Bruno de Hezeta is possibly the first European to set foot in Oregon.
1792	American captain Robert Gray enters and names the Columbia River.
1805	The Corps of Discovery sails down the Snake and Columbia rivers to the Pacific Ocean.
1811	John Jacob Astor's expeditions set up a trading settlement at the mouth of the Columbia River.
1818	The United States and Britain agree to share the Oregon Country.
1843	The first Champoeg Meeting is held.
1845	About three thousand "overlanders" arrive in the Oregon Country.
1848	The Oregon Territory is formed.
1859	Oregon becomes the thirty-third state admitted to the Union.
1883	The first tracks connect Portland to the transcontinental railroad.
1902	The Oregon Legislative Assembly approves the Oregon System; Crater Lake National Park opens.
1912	The Marmot Dam is completed on Sandy River, a tributary to the Columbia River.
1913	Oregon beaches are declared public land.
1938	The first dam on the Columbia River is completed.
1971	The Oregon Bottle Bill is approved.
1991	Barbara Roberts becomes the first woman governor of Oregon.
2007	The Marmot Dam is removed to help heal the surrounding environment.
2008	Portland tops Sustain Line's list of the fifty most environmentally sustainable American cities.

Oregon at a Glance

State motto	*Alis volat propriis* ("She flies with her own wings.")
State capital	Salem
State song	"Oregon, My Oregon"
State flower	Oregon grape
State bird	Western meadowlark
State tree	Douglas fir
State fruit	Pear
Statehood date and number	February 14, 1859; thirty-third state
State nickname	Beaver State
Total area and U.S. rank	98,466 square miles (255,026 sq km); ninth-largest state
Population	3,747,000
Length of coastline	362 miles (583 km)
Highest elevation	Mount Hood, at 11,249 feet (3,429 m)

State Flag

State Seal

Lowest elevation	Pacific coast, at 0 feet (0 m)
Major rivers	Columbia River, Deschutes River, Willamette River, John Day River, Snake River
Major lakes	Upper Klamath Lake, Crater Lake
Hottest recorded temperature	119 degrees Fahrenheit (48 degrees Celsius) in Pendleton, on August 10, 1898
Coldest recorded temperature	-54°F (-12°C) in Seneca, on February 10, 1933
Origin of state name	May be from the Native American words for "beautiful river."
Chief agricultural products	Potatoes, wheat, hazelnuts, cherries, berries, tree fruits, onions, corn
Major industries	Service industries, technological industries, logging, agriculture, fishing

State Bird

State Flower

GLOSSARY

bicameral Having two separate lawmaking assemblies, such as the Senate and House of Representatives in Congress.

caldera A large crater in a volcano formed by a collapse of the walls that form the volcano's cone.

commissioner A governmental representative in an administrative role.

commodity An item that is bought and sold, especially an unprocessed item.

conservation The protection and care of natural resources.

council-manager government A system of local government that combines an elected council of officials with an appointed local government manager (or mayor).

direct legislation A form of government that gives voters more say in the laws that are made.

elevation The height above sea level.

estuary The area where a freshwater river or stream mixes with saltwater tides, forming a unique ecological region.

fescue A grass grown for lawns and as feed for livestock.

geologist A scientist who studies Earth's structure and processes.

gorge A deep, narrow, rocky valley.

gross state product A measurement of the economic output of a state.

ice age A geological period when global temperature drops and glaciers cover much of Earth.

marionberry A type of blackberry commonly grown in Oregon.

plateau A hill or mountain with a flat top.

progressive Advocating social or political reform.

ratify To give formal approval to something.

spawn To produce and deposit eggs, as in fish.

veto The power of the executive branch to reject the legislation of another branch.

FOR MORE INFORMATION

Center for Columbia River History

1109 East 5th Street

Vancouver, WA 98661

(360) 258-3289

Web site: http://www.ccrh.org

This association of the Washington State Historical Society, Portland State University, and Washington State University–Vancouver promotes the study of Columbia River Basin history.

Clackamas Heritage Partners

1726 Washington Street

Oregon City, OR 97045

(503) 657-9336

Web site: http://www.historicoregoncity.org

Clackamas Heritage Partners directs and coordinates historic sites in Oregon City, including the Museum of the Oregon Territory.

Oregon Coast Visitors Association (OCVA)

137 NE First Street

P.O. Box 74

Newport, OR 97365

(888) OCVA-101 (628-2101)

Web site: http://visittheoregoncoast.com

The OCVA works with chambers of congress of coastal towns to promote vacation travel, recreation, attractions, and overnight stays on Oregon's coast.

Oregon Historical Society

1200 SW Park Avenue

Portland, OR 97205

(503) 306-5198

Web site: http://www.ohs.org

According to its Web site, the Oregon Historical Society's mission is "preserving and interpreting Oregon's past in thoughtful, illuminating, and provocative ways."

Oregon State University

2900 SW Jefferson Way

Corvallis, OR 97331-4501

(541) 737-1000

Web site: http://oregonstate.edu

Oregon State University is a land grant institution that promotes economic, social, cultural, and environmental progress for the people of Oregon and the United States.

Willamette Riverkeeper

1515 SE Water Avenue, #102

Portland, OR 97214

(503) 223-6418

Web site: http://www.willamette-riverkeeper.org

This association is dedicated to the protection and restoration of the Willamette River.

Web Sites

Due to the changing nature of Internet links, Rosen Publishing has developed an online list of Web sites related to the subject of this book. This site is updated regularly. Please use this link to access this list:

http://www.rosenlinks.com/uspp/orpp

FOR FURTHER READING

Ambrose, Stephen. *Undaunted Courage: Meriwether Lewis, Thomas Jefferson, and the Opening of the American West.* 1st ed. New York, NY: Simon & Schuster, 1997.

Bishop, Ellen Morris. *In Search of Ancient Oregon: A Geological and Natural History.* Portland, OR: Timber Press, 2006.

Bodden, Valerie. *Oregon* (This Land Called America). Mankato, MN: Creative Education, 2009.

Eisenberg, Jana. *Lewis and Clark: Path to the Pacific.* New York, NY: Children's Press, 2008.

Engeman, Richard H. *The Oregon Companion: An Historical Gazetteer of the Useful, the Curious, and the Arcane.* Portland, OR: Timber Press, 2009.

Hermes, Patricia. *Westward to Home: Joshua's Oregon Trail Diary.* New York, NY: Scholastic, 2002.

Kent, Deborah. *Oregon.* New York, NY: Children's Press, 2009.

Landau, Elaine. *The Oregon Trail.* New York, NY: Scholastic, 2006.

Lewis, Meriwether, and William Clark. *The Journals of Lewis and Clark.* New York, NY: Signet Classics, 2004.

Marschner, Janice. *Oregon 1859: A Snapshot in Time.* Portland, OR: Timber Press, 2008.

Marsh, Carole. *Oregon Indians.* Peachtree City, GA: Gallopade International, 2004.

McNeese, Tim. *The Oregon Trail: Pathway to the West.* New York, NY: Chelsea House Publishers, 2009.

Middleton, David, and Rod Barbee. *The Photographer's Guide to the Oregon Coast: Where to Find Perfect Shots and How to Take Them.* Woodstock, VT: Countryman Press, 2004.

Peterson Del Mar, David. *Oregon's Promise: An Interpretive History.* Corvallis, OR: Oregon State University Press, 2003.

Pintarich, Dick. *Great and Minor Moments in Oregon History: An Illustrated Anthology of Illuminating Glimpses into Oregon's Past—From Prehistory to the Present.* Portland, OR: New Oregon Publishers, 2006.

Rife, Douglas M. *History Speaks: Chief Joseph Surrenders.* Dayton, OH: Teaching and Learning Co., 2002.

Ruth, Amy. *Herbert Hoover.* Minneapolis, MN: Learner Publications, 2004.

Shannon, Terry Miller. *Oregon.* New York, NY: Children's Press, 2009.

Stewart, Mark. *The Portland Trail Blazers.* Chicago, IL: Norwood House Press, 2007.

Van Leeuwen, Jean. *Bound for Oregon.* New York, NY: Penguin Books, 1996.

BIBLIOGRAPHY

Animal Planet. "Meet Terri and Bindi." Discovery.com. Retrieved February 26, 2009 (http://animal.discovery.com/tv/planets-best/terri-bindi/terri-bindi_02.html).

BeverlyCleary.com. "The World of Beverly Cleary." Retrieved February 26, 2009 (http://www.beverlycleary.com/beverlycleary/index.html).

Biographybase.com. "Danny Ainge Biography." Retrieved February 26, 2009 (http://www.biographybase.com/biography/Ainge_Danny.html).

Biography Channel. "River Phoenix." A&E. Retrieved February 26, 2009 (http://www.thebiographychannel.co.uk/biography_story/604:719/1/River_Phoenix.htm).

Chocano, Carina. "Matt Groening." Salon.com, January 30, 2001. Retrieved February 26, 2009 (http://archive.salon.com/people/bc/2001/01/30/groening).

Hart, Joyce. *Oregon*. Tarrytown, NY: Marshall Cavendish Benchmark, 2006.

Kent, Deborah. *Oregon*. New York, NY: Children's Press, 2009.

Lambiek. "Carl Banks." Comiclopedia. Retrieved February 12, 2009 (http://lambiek.net/artists/b/barks.htm).

Linus Pauling Institute. "Linus Pauling Biography." Oregon State University. Retrieved February 12, 2009 (http://lpi.oregonstate.edu/lpbio/lpbio2.html).

MSNBC.com. "Ann Curry." October 1, 2008. Retrieved February 26, 2009 (http://www.msnbc.msn.com/id/8418780).

Netstate.com. "The Geography of Oregon." September 18, 2008. Retrieved February 28, 2009 (http://www.netstate.com/states/geography/or_geography.htm).

Oregon Department of Agriculture. "Growing Regions in Oregon." Oregon.gov, May 13, 2008. Retrieved February 25, 2009 (http://oregon.gov/ODA/regions.shtml).

Oregon Department of Agriculture. "2007–2008 Oregon Agriculture & Fisheries Statistics." Oregon.gov. Retrieved March 2, 2009 (http://www.oregon.gov/ODA/pub_agripedia.shtml).

Oregon State Legislature. "State Motto Timeline." Retrieved February 26, 2009 (http://www.leg.state.or.us/history/motto.htm).

Oregon State University. "Oregon Production." November 3, 2008. Retrieved February 28, 2009 (http://oregonstate.edu/potatoes/orprod.htm).

PBS.org. "Chief Joseph." New Perspectives on the West. Retrieved February 26, 2009 (http://www.pbs.org/weta/thewest/people/a_c/chiefjoseph.htm).

Salem Online History. "Herbert Hoover: Three Important Years in Marion County." Retrieved February 26, 2009 (http://www.salemhistory.net/people/herbert_hoover.htm).

Shannon, Terry Miller. *Oregon*. New York, NY: Children's Press, 2009.

Stefoff, Rebecca. *Oregon*. Tarrytown, NY: Marshall Cavendish Benchmark, 2006.

University of Oregon. "The World's Oldest Shoes." Retrieved February 12, 2009 (http://www.uoregon.edu/~connolly/FRsandals.htm).

U.S. Environmental Protection Agency. "Willamette Basin Alternative Futures Analysis." August 2002. Retrieved February 15, 2009 (http://www.epa.gov/wed/pages/projects/alternativefutures/twopager.pdf).

Willamette Riverkeeper. "River History." Retrieved March 2, 2009 (http://www.willamette-riverkeeper.org/WRK/riverhistory.html).

Yamaka, Julie, ed. *Oregon Blue Book*. Salem, OR: Oregon State Archives, 2009.

INDEX

About the Author

Greg Roza has written and edited educational materials for children for the past eight years. He has a master's degree in English from the State University of New York at Fredonia. Roza has long had an interest in scientific topics, and spends much of his spare time tinkering with machines around the house. He lives in Hamburg, New York, with his wife, Abigail, and his three children, Autumn, Lincoln, and Daisy.

Photo Credits

Cover (top left) American Stock/Hulton Archive/Getty Images; cover (top right) scphotos/Newscom; cover (bottom) © www.istockphoto.com/Zhifeng Wang; pp. 3, 6, 13, 20, 21, 26, 32, 38, 40 Wikimedia Commons; p. 4 (top) © GeoAtlas; p. 7 Shutterstock.com; p. 10 John Giustina/Taxi/Getty Images; p. 11 © www.istockphoto.com/Julie Flavin; p. 15 Independence National Historical Park; p. 16 Hulton Archive/Getty Images; p. 18 Photo Researchers, Inc.; p. 24 Oregon State Archives, Oregon Provisional/Territorial Government, #406; p. 27 © Wildlife/Peter Arnold, Inc.; p. 29 © Peter Chigmaroff/Alamy; p. 30 © AP Images; p. 33 Kevin Winter/Getty Images; p. 34 MPI/Hulton Archive/Getty Images; p. 35 Stock Montage/Hulton Archive/Getty Images; p. 36 Pictorial Parade/Hulton Archive/Getty Images; p. 39 (left) Courtesy of Robesus Inc.

Designer: Les Kanturek; Editor: Nicholas Croce;
Photo Researcher: Cindy Reiman